Our

HENRI J. M. NOUWEN

Our Greatest Gift

A Meditation on Dying and Caring

HarperOne
An Imprint of HarperCollinsPublishers

HarperOne

OUR GREATEST GIFT: A *Meditation on Dying and Caring*.
Copyright © 1994 by Henri J. M. Nouwen.
All rights reserved.
Printed in the United States of America.
No part of this book may be used or reproduced in
any manner whatsoever without written
permission except in the case of
brief quotations embodied in
critical articles and reviews.
For information address HarperCollins Publishers,
195 Broadway, New York, NY 10007.

FIRST HARPERCOLLINS PAPERBACK EDITION PUBLISHED IN 1995

Designed by Greta D. Sibley

Library of Congress Cataloging-in-Publication Data
Nouwen, Henri J. M.
Our greatest gift: a meditation on dying and caring /
Henri J. M. Nouwen. p. cm.
ISBN 978–0–06–180026–9
1. Death—Religious aspects—Christianity.
2. Nouwen, Henri J. M. 3. Spiritual life—Catholic authors.
I. Title.
BT825.N685 1994
242'.4—dc20

22 LSC(C) 20 19 18 17 16 15

To Marina Nouwen-San Giorgi,
my sister-in-law,
whose courage and joy
were a great inspiration.
She died in the early morning of
May 8, 1993.
May this book honor her.

CONTENTS

ACKNOWLEDGMENTS   ix

PROLOGUE
Befriending Death   xi

INTRODUCTION
Grace Hidden in Powerlessness   1

PART ONE: DYING WELL   7

Close to the Heart   9

CHAPTER ONE
We Are Children of God   11

CHAPTER TWO
We Are Brothers and Sisters of Each Other   21

CHAPTER THREE
We Are Parents of Generations to Come   31

The Choice to Die Well   45

PART TWO: CARING WELL   47

At the Heart of Being Human   49

CHAPTER FOUR
You Are a Child of God   51

CHAPTER FIVE
You Are Brothers and Sisters of Each Other   65

CHAPTER SIX
You Are Parents of Generations to Come   81

The Choice to Care Well   95

CONCLUSION
The Grace of the Resurrection   97

EPILOGUE
Death: A Loss and a Gift   105

ACKNOWLEDGMENTS

THIS LITTLE BOOK would never have been written without the warm friendship and generous hospitality of my German friends Franz and Reny Johna. In their home, I found not only a quiet place to write, but also the lively company to discuss my thoughts and bounce off my ideas. My gratitude to them is deep and lasting.

I also thank all the friends who are mentioned in this book. Not only did they allow me to write about them, but many took the time to critically read the manuscript and make suggestions for changes and additions.

A special word of thanks goes to my secretary, Kathy Christie, for typing and retyping the text and for offering me much-needed encouragement and support during the final phases of writing this book. I am also grateful for Conrad Wieczorek's and Terri Goff's careful editing work.

Finally I want to express my deep gratitude to Peggy McDonnell, her family, and friends. Their faithful encouragement and generous financial support in memory of Murray McDonnell have enabled me to find the quiet time and space to write *Our Greatest Gift*.

—Henri J. M. Nouwen

Befriending Death

ON DECEMBER 31, 1992, at three o'clock in the afternoon, Maurice Gould died. He died in York Central Hospital in Richmond Hill, near Toronto, Canada, after a long struggle with Alzheimer's disease.

Maurice — "Moe," as we called him — had been a member of L'Arche. Founded in 1964 by the Canadian Jean Vanier, L'Arche is a worldwide network of communities where people with mental disabilities and their assistants create home for one another. Maurice had made his home in the L'Arche Daybreak community in Toronto for fourteen years. He was known for his joyfulness, gentleness, and love of home. The countless people who met him over the years speak about him with much endearment. Somehow his condition —

Down's syndrome—seemed only the other side of his great gift: to give and receive love.

During the last days of Moe's life, I was in Freiburg, Germany. Daybreak had sent me there to take a few months away from my pastoral work in the community and focus exclusively on my writing. When Nathan Ball, the director of our community, called me to tell me about Moe's death, I knew at once that I must return to Toronto as soon as possible to be with Moe's family and many friends and to experience with them the sorrow of his leaving, as well as the joy of his fifty-eight fulfilling years of life.

The next day, during my flight home, I thought a great deal about life and death and began to wonder how our dying can be as much our own as our living.

As the Air Canada plane took me from Frankfurt over Germany, Holland, England, the Atlantic Ocean, and Nova Scotia, Canada, to Toronto, I had ample time to think about dying: Maurice's dying, my own dying, and the dying of so many people every day all over the world.

Is death something so terrible and absurd that we are better off not thinking or talking about it? Is death such an undesirable part of our existence that we are better off acting as if it were not real? Is death such an absolute end of all our thoughts and actions that we simply cannot face it? Or is it possible to befriend our dying gradually and live open to it, trusting that we have nothing to fear? Is it possible to prepare for our death with the same attentiveness that our parents had in preparing for our birth? Can we wait for our death as for a friend who wants to welcome us home?

During the eight-and-one-half-hour flight, I thought not only about Maurice and these questions, but also about my other dying friends and my aging father. Just over a month earlier, on November 24, I had been with Rick in Bethany House, the Catholic worker house in Oakland, California. Bethany House was recently founded by Michael Harank to provide a place to care for people living with AIDS. Rick has AIDS and knows that he has only a short time left to live. As I sat on his bed and held his hand, he said, "What can I still do in the months that are left to me? My friend, who I love so much, can make all sorts of plans for his future, but I have no future anymore." Tears flowed from his eyes as he tightened his grip on my hand.

Then I thought of Marina, my sister-in-law, who had struggled for five full years with intestinal cancer, had survived three horrendous surgeries, and finally, when all further therapy had proved useless, had allowed things to take their natural course. Marina had spoken openly about her death to her doctors, to the nurses, to her many friends, to her mother, to her husband, Paul, and to me. In her poems, she had expressed her feelings about her approaching death, even while those around her hardly dared mention it in her presence.

Meanwhile, my father, in Holland, would celebrate his ninetieth birthday within ten days. He is full of energy, still writing, still lecturing, still making plans. But to me he says, "Son, my body is spent, my eyes are no longer able to focus, my stomach doesn't tolerate much food anymore, and my heart is very, very weak."

People are dying. Not just the few I know, but countless people everywhere, every day, every hour. Dying is the most general human event, something we all have to do. But do we do it well? Is our death more than an unavoidable fate that we simply wish would not be? Can it somehow become an act of fulfillment, perhaps more human than any other human act?

When I arrived that day in January at Terminal II at Pearson International Airport in Toronto, Nathan Ball was waiting for me. In the car, he told me about Moe's death. Family and friends had been with Moe during his last hours. Both sadness and gladness had been there. A beautiful friend had left us. A long suffering had come to a gentle end. "Moe was so much loved by everyone," Nathan said. "We will miss him, but it was time for him to go."

The days that followed were full of sorrow and joy. Moe was dead, but it seemed as if new life became immediately visible. Telephone calls were made to friends far and wide; letters were written. Most of all, people came together to pray, to eat, to tell stories, to look at pictures—to remember with smiles and tears. Of all the days that I have lived at Daybreak, those after Moe's death belong to the most intimate, the most uniting, and, in a strange way, the most sacred. A man who, through his fragility and weakness, had helped us create community during his life did so even more through his death. As we came together in our chapel, visited the funeral home, sang and spoke in gratitude in the Anglican Church of Richmond Hill, and carried the coffin to the grave in King City's cemetery, we shared a deep sense that not only does life lead to death, but death leads to new life. The spirit of gentleness and kindness that surrounded and pervaded our conversation, the spirit of forgiveness and healing that touched each of us, and most of all the spirit of unity and communion that bound us together in a new way—that spirit was gratefully received as a gift of Moe, who was dead and yet very much alive.

On the evening before my return to Europe to celebrate my father's birthday and to continue my writing in Freiburg, I had dinner with Nathan, a friend and longtime member of Daybreak, and Sue Mosteller. During the meal, Nathan asked me, "Where and how do you want to die?" He raised the question in a gentle way. It was a question that came from our new awareness that, like Moe, we would soon die. Our awareness prompted us to ask ourselves: Are we preparing ourselves for our death, or are we ignoring death by keeping busy? Are we helping each other to die, or do we simply assume we are going to always be here for each other? Will our death give new life, new hope, and new faith to our friends, or will it be no more than another cause for sadness? The main question is not, How much will we still be able to do during the few years we have left to live? but rather, How can we prepare ourselves for our death in such a way that our dying will be a new way for us to send our and God's spirit to those whom we have loved and who have loved us?

Nathan's question, "Where and how do you want to die?" brought me face-to-face with a great challenge: not only to live well, but also to die well.

The next day, as we drove to the airport, Nathan thanked me for returning for Moe's funeral and wished me a happy celebration of my father's birthday and a creative month of writing in Freiburg. While flying to Amsterdam, I realized that I knew better than before what I would write about. I wanted to write about befriending my death so that it can become my best gift to the world I love so much.

Now—after many celebrations in Holland and a long train ride through Germany—I am alone again in my little, peaceful, and solitary apartment in Freiburg. What better place than this in which to befriend death?

INTRODUCTION

Grace Hidden in Powerlessness

IT HAS NEVER BEEN EASY for me to find a quiet place to write. I have gone to convents, monasteries, and retreat centers and have even tried to stay home with the door closed. But wherever I have searched for solitude, I have soon become entangled again in the daily events of my surroundings. My own restlessness, my need for companionship, and my fear of rejection and abandonment have made me flee solitude as soon as I have found it. My resistance to solitude has proved as strong as my desire for it. Again and again I have found excuses to talk with people, give conferences, preach sermons, preside at liturgies, join in celebrations, or hang around in libraries. In short, I have found excuses not to be alone.

Still, I have always known that one day I would have to find the courage to go beyond my fear. I would have to trust that in solitude I would discover my true teacher, who would give me the words that I must write.

Now I have my chance. Franz and Reny Johna, my friends in Freiburg, have offered me the third story of their three-story house in the Schubert Strasse. The first story serves as their own home, the second is rented to an elderly couple, and the third is usually kept free for their two children, Robert and Irene. Robert, however, has moved to the United States, where he specializes in internal medicine, and Irene has moved to Frankfurt, where she works for the Bundesbank. "You can have the third-story apartment," Franz and Reny said to me. "It is a true hermitage, away from people and the events of every day, and definitely noise- and light-proof." Indeed, the third story of Franz and Reny's house is the ideal place for a city hermit. It has everything a solitary person can desire: a study, a bedroom, a small living room that I have made into a kitchen, and a bathroom.

So now I have what I have always dreamed of having: complete silence, complete solitude. When I let down the window blinds, my bedroom is pitch dark, and not even the sound of a passing car can be heard. All becomes completely still.

This stillness is purifying. Strange as it may seem, the outer quietude quickly reveals the inner restlessness. What am I going to do when there is nothing to do? What am I going to do when there is no one demanding my attention or inviting me to do something or making me feel valuable? Without phone calls, letters, and meetings, the minutes, hours, and days stretch out into horizonless deserts of solitude.

Is this not the most blessed place in which to befriend my death? Is this not the place where the outer silence can gradually lead me to an inner silence, where I can embrace my own mortality? Yes, silence and solitude invite me to gradually let go of the outer voices that give me a sense of well-being among my fellow humans, to trust the inner voice that reveals to me my true name. Silence and solitude call me to detach myself from the scaffolding of daily life and to discover if anything there can stand on its own when the traditional support systems have been pulled away.

While sitting alone in my little hermitage, I realize how unprepared I am to die. The silence and solitude of this comfortable apartment are sufficient to make me aware of my unwillingness to let go of life. Nevertheless, I will have to die soon. The ten, twenty, or thirty years left to me will fly by quickly. Gradually, my body will lose its strength, my mind its flexibility; I will lose family and friends; I will become less relevant to society and be forgotten by most; I will have to depend increasingly on the help of others; and, in the end, I will have to let go of everything and be carried into the completely unknown.

Am I willing to make that journey? Am I willing to let go of whatever power I have left, to unclench my fists and trust in the grace hidden in complete powerlessness? I don't know. I really don't know. It seems impossible, since everything alive in me protests against this journey into nothingness. I do know that the silence and solitude of my small apartment in Freiburg offer me the best opportunity I will ever have to explore my ability to surrender to death.

Somehow, I believe that this lonely task of befriending my death is not simply a task that serves me, but also a task that may serve others. I have lived my whole life with the desire to help others in their journey, but I have always realized that I had little else to offer than my own, the journey I am making myself. How can I announce joy, peace, forgiveness, and reconciliation unless they are part of my own flesh and blood? I have always wanted to be a good shepherd for others, but I have always known, too, that good shepherds lay down their own lives—their pains and joys, their doubts and hopes, their fears and their love—for their friends.

Now in my sixties, trying to come to terms with my own mortality, I trust that, like everything else I have lived, my attempt to befriend my death will be good not only for me, but also for others who face a similar challenge. I want to die well, but I desire also to help others to die well. In this way, I am not alone in my little apartment in the Schubert Strasse in Freiburg. In fact, I am surrounded by people who are dying and who hope to die well. I want my silence and solitude to be for my friends and for the friends of my friends. I want my desire to embrace my own mortality to help others embrace theirs. I want my little hermitage to be truly in and for the world.

I have five weeks ahead of me in this sanctuary: five weeks in which to pray, to think, and to write about dying and death—my own as well as that of others. My task has two sides to it. First, I must discover what it means to befriend my own death. Second, I must discover how I can help others befriend theirs. The inner life is always a life for others. When I myself am able to befriend death, I will be able to help others do the same. That is the work of this little book. I write first about dying well, then about caring well.

PART ONE

———

DYING WELL

Close to the Heart

AS CHILDREN, we need parents, teachers, and friends to teach us the meaning of our lives. Once we have grown up, we are on our own. Then, we ourselves become the main source of knowledge, and what we say to others about life and death has to come from what is truly our own. Great thinkers and great saints have written and spoken about dying and death, but their words remain uniquely theirs. I must find my own words so that what I say comes from the depth of my experience. Although many people have deeply influenced that experience, nobody else has had it. In this lies its power, but in this too lies its weakness. I must trust that my experience of mortality will give me words that can speak to others who are struggling to give meaning to their own lives and deaths. I must also accept that many will not be able to respond to what I have to say, simply because they cannot see or feel the connections between their lives and mine.

In the first three chapters of this book, I deal with dying well. I explore in my own innermost being what it means that we human beings are children of God, brothers and sisters of each other, and parents of generations to come.

I stay close to my own heart, listening carefully to what I have heard and felt. I also stay close to the hearts of those whose joys and pains are touching me most at this time of my life. Most of all, I stay close to the heart of Jesus, whose life and death are the main source for understanding and living my own life and death.

CHAPTER ONE

We Are Children of God

WHEN I BECAME SIXTY, the Daybreak community gave me a big party. More than one hundred people came together to celebrate. John Bloss was there, eager as always to play an active role. John is full of good thoughts, but his disability makes it painfully difficult for him to express these thoughts in words. Still, he loves to speak, especially when he has a captive audience.

With everyone sitting in a large circle, Joe, the master of ceremonies, said, "Well, John, what do you have to say to Henri today?" John, who loves the theatrical, got up, put himself in the center of the circle, pointed to me, and began to search for words. "You . . . you . . . are," he said with a big grin on his face. "You . . . you . . . are . . . uh . . . uh . . ." Everyone looked at him with great expectation as he tried to get his words out while pointing ever-more directly at me. "You . . . you . . . are . . . uh . . . uh . . ." And then, like an explosion, the words came out. "An old man!" Everybody burst out laughing, and John basked in the success of his performance.

That said it all. I had become "an old man." Few people would say it so directly, and most would continue with qualifications about still looking young, still so full of energy, and on and on. John said it simply and truthfully: "You are an old man."

It seems fair to say that people between the ages of one and thirty are considered young; those between thirty and sixty are considered middle-aged; and those past their sixtieth birthday are considered old. But then you yourself are suddenly sixty, and you don't feel old. At least I don't. My teenage years seem only a short time ago, my years of studying and teaching feel like yesterday, and my seven years at Daybreak feel like seven days. Thinking of myself as "an old man" does not come spontaneously. I need to hear it announced loud and clear.

A few years ago a university student spoke to me about his father. "My dad doesn't understand me," he said. "He's so bossy, and he always wants to be right; he never allows any room for my ideas. It's difficult to be with him." Trying to comfort him, I said, "My dad is not very different from yours, but, you know, that's the older generation!" Then with a sigh, he said, "Yes, my dad is already forty!" I suddenly realized that I was speaking to someone who could have been my grandson.

Indeed, I somehow keep forgetting that I have become old and that young people regard me as an old man. It helps me to look at myself in a mirror once in a while. Gazing at my face, I see both my mother and my father when they were sixty years old, and I remember how I thought of them as old people.

Being an old man means being close to death. In the past, I often tried to figure out if I could still double the years I had lived. When I was twenty, I was sure that I would live at least another twenty years. When I was thirty, I trusted that I would easily reach sixty. When I was forty, I wondered if I would make it to eighty. And when I turned fifty, I realized that only a few make it to one hundred. But now, at sixty, I am sure that I have gone far past the halfway point and that my death is much closer to me than my birth.

Old men and old women must prepare for death. But how do we prepare ourselves well? For me, the first task is to become a child again—to reclaim my childhood. This might seem to be opposite to our natural desire to maintain maximum independence. Nevertheless, becoming a child—entering a second childhood—is essential to dying a good death. Jesus spoke about this second childhood when he said, "Unless you change and become like little children, you will never enter the Kingdom of Heaven" (Matthew 18:3).

What characterizes this second childhood? It has to do with a new dependence. For the first twenty or so years of life, we depend on our parents, teachers, and friends. Forty years later, we again become increasingly dependent. The younger we are, the more people we need so that we may live; the older we become, the more people we again need to live. Life is lived from dependence to dependence.

That's the mystery that God has revealed to us through Jesus, whose life was a journey from the manger to the cross. Born in complete dependence on those who surrounded him, Jesus died as the passive victim of other people's actions and decisions. His was the journey from the first to the second childhood. He came as a child and died as a child, and he lived his life so that we may claim and reclaim our own childhood and thus make our death—as he did his—into a new birth.

I have been blessed with an experience that has made all of this clear to me. A few years ago, I was hit by a car while walking along a roadside and brought to the hospital with a ruptured spleen. The doctor told me she wasn't sure that I would make it through surgery. I did, but the hours lived before and after the operation allowed me to get in touch with my childhood as never before. Bound with straps on a table that looked like a cross, surrounded by masked figures, I experienced my complete dependence. I realized not only that I fully depended on the skills of an unknown medical team, but also that my deepest being was a dependent being. I knew with a certainty that had nothing to do with any particular human insight that, whether or not I survived the surgery, I was safely held in a divine embrace and would certainly live.

This freak accident had led me into a childlike state in which I needed to be cared for as a helpless infant, an experience that offered me an immense sense of safety—the experience of being a child of God. All at once, I knew that all human dependencies are embedded in a divine dependence and that that divine dependence makes dying part of a greater and much vaster way of living. This experience was so real, so basic, and so all-pervasive that it changed radically my sense of self and affected profoundly my state of consciousness. There is a strange paradox here: dependence on people often leads to slavery, but dependence on God leads to freedom. When we know that God holds us safely—whatever happens—we don't have to fear anything or anyone but can walk through life with great confidence. This is a radical perspective; we are accustomed to thinking of the ways in which people are oppressed and exploited as signs of their dependence and therefore perceive of true freedom only as the result of independence. We can think about this in another way, however. When we claim our most intimate dependence on God not as a curse but as a gift, then we can discover the freedom of the children of God. This deep inner freedom allows us to confront our enemies, throw off the yoke of oppression, and build social and economic structures that allow us to live as brothers and sisters, as children of the one God whose name is love. This, I believe, is the way in which Jesus spoke about freedom. It is the freedom rooted in being a child of God.

We are fearful people. We are afraid of conflict, war, an uncertain future, illness, and, most of all, death. This fear takes away our freedom and gives our society the power to manipulate us with threats and promises. When we can reach beyond our fears to the One who loves us with a love that was there before we were born and will be there after we die, then oppression, persecution, and even death will be unable to take our freedom. Once we have come to the deep inner knowledge—a knowledge more of the heart than of the mind—that we are born out of love and will die into love, that every part of our being is deeply rooted in love and that this love is our true Father and Mother, then all forms of evil, illness, and death lose their final

power over us and become painful but hopeful reminders of our true divine childhood. The apostle Paul
expressed this experience of the complete freedom of
the children of God when he wrote, "I am certain of
this: neither death nor life, nor angels, nor principali-
ties, nothing already in existence and nothing still to
come, nor any power, nor the heights nor the depths,
nor any created thing whatever, will be able to come
between us and the love of God, known to us in Christ
Jesus" (Romans 8:38–39).

So the first tasks in preparing ourselves for death
are to claim the freedom of the children of God and,
in so doing, to strip death of any further power over
us. The word *child* has its problems. It suggests little-
ness, weakness, naïveté, and immaturity. But when I
say that we must grow into a second childhood, I do
not mean a second immaturity. To the contrary, I think
of the maturity of the sons and daughters of God, of
the sons and daughters chosen to inherit the Kingdom.
There is nothing little, weak, or naïve about being a
child of God. In fact, this election allows us to keep
our heads erect in the presence of God even while we
walk through a world falling apart on every side. As
sons and daughters of God, we can walk through the
gates of death with the self-confidence of heirs. Paul
again proclaimed this loudly as he said, "All who are
guided by the Spirit of God are sons [and daughters] of

God: for what you received was not the spirit of slavery to bring you back into fear; you have received the spirit of adoption, enabling us to cry out, 'Abba, Father.' The Spirit himself joins with our spirit to bear witness that we are children of God. And if we are children, then we are heirs, heirs of God and joint-heirs with Christ, provided we share his suffering, so as to share his glory" (Romans 8:14–17).

This is not the voice of a small, timid child. This is the voice of a spiritually mature person who knows that he is in the presence of God and for whom complete dependence on God has become the source of strength, the basis of courage, and the secret of true inner freedom.

Recently, a friend told me a story about twins talking to each other in the womb. The sister said to the brother, "I believe there is life after birth." Her brother protested vehemently, "No, no, this is all there is. This is a dark and cozy place, and we have nothing else to do but to cling to the cord that feeds us." The little girl insisted, "There must be something more than this dark place. There must be something else, a place with light where there is freedom to move." Still, she could not convince her twin brother.

After some silence, the sister said hesitantly, "I have something else to say, and I'm afraid you won't believe that, either, but I think there is a mother." Her brother became furious. "A mother!" he shouted. "What are you talking about? I have never seen a mother, and neither have you. Who put that idea in your head? As I told you, this place is all we have. Why do you always want more? This is not such a bad place, after all. We have all we need, so let's be content."

The sister was quite overwhelmed by her brother's response and for a while didn't dare say anything more. But she couldn't let go of her thoughts, and since she had only her twin brother to speak to, she finally said, "Don't you feel these squeezes every once in a while? They're quite unpleasant and sometimes even painful." "Yes," he answered. "What's special about that?" "Well," the sister said, "I think that these squeezes are there to get us ready for another place, much more beautiful than this, where we will see our mother face-to-face. Don't you think that's exciting?"

The brother didn't answer. He was fed up with the foolish talk of his sister and felt that the best thing would be simply to ignore her and hope that she would leave him alone.

This story may help us to think about death in a new way. We can live as if this life were all we had, as if death were absurd and we had better not talk about it; or we can choose to claim our divine childhood and trust that death is the painful but blessed passage that will bring us face-to-face with our God.

CHAPTER TWO

We Are Brothers and Sisters of Each Other

TWO OF THE GREATEST JOYS experienced are the joy of being different from others and the joy of being the same as others. The first of these I saw while watching the 1992 Summer Olympics in Barcelona on television. Those who stood on the rostrum and received their bronze, silver, and gold medals experienced joy as the direct result of being able to run faster, jump higher, or throw farther than others. The difference might have been extremely small, but it had great significance. It was the distinction between defeat and victory, between rueful tears and ecstatic joy. This is the joy of the hero and the star, the joy that comes from successfully competing, winning the prize, receiving the honor, and walking into the limelight.

I know this joy myself. I know it from getting an award at school, from being chosen the leader of my class, from receiving tenure at the university, and from seeing my books published and receiving honorary degrees. I know the immense satisfaction that comes from being considered different from others. These types of achievements dispel self-doubts and bestow self-confidence. This is the joy of having "made it," the joy of being recognized for making a difference. We all wait for this joy somewhere, somehow. It remains the joy of the one who said, "I thank you God, that I am not like everyone else" (Luke 18:11–12).

The other kind of joy is harder to describe but easier to find. It is the joy of being the brother or sister of all people. Although this joy is closer at hand—more accessible—than the joy of being different, it is not as obvious, and only a few people ever truly find it. This is the joy of being a part of that vast variety of people —of all ages, colors, and religions—who together form the human family. This is the immense joy of being a member of the human race.

At several times in my life, I have tasted this joy. I felt it most acutely in 1964, when I walked with thousands of people in Alabama from Selma to Montgomery in a civil rights march led by Martin Luther King, Jr. I will never forget the joy I experienced during that march. I had come by myself. Nobody knew me—nobody had ever heard of me—but when we walked together and put our arms around each other's shoulders and sang "We shall overcome one day," I experienced a joy I had never experienced before in my life. I said to myself, "Yes, yes, I belong; these are my people. They may have a differently colored skin, a different religion, a different way of life, but they are my brothers and sisters. They love me, and I love them. Their smiles and tears are my smiles and tears; their prayers and prophecies are my prayers and prophecies; their anguish and hope are my anguish and hope. I am one with them."

In an instant, all differences seemed to melt away as snow in the sun. All my comparing disappeared, and I felt surrounded by the welcoming arms of all humanity. I was aware that some of the people with whom I held hands had spent years in prison, were addicted to drugs or alcohol, suffered from loneliness and depression, and lived lives radically different from mine, but they all looked to me like saints, radiant with God's love. They were indeed God's people, immensely loved and radically forgiven. All I felt was a deep sameness, a profound communion with all people, an exhilarating sense of brotherhood and sisterhood.

I am convinced that it is this joy—the joy of being the same as others, of belonging to one human family—that allows us to die well. I do not know how I or anyone else could be prepared to die if we were mainly concerned about the trophies we had collected during our best years. The great gift hidden in our dying is the gift of unity with all people. However different we are, we were all born powerless, and we all die powerless, and the little differences we live in between dwindle in the light of this enormous truth. Often this human truth is presented as a reason to be sad. It is not seldom called a "sobering truth." Our great challenge is to discover this truth as a source of immense joy that will set us free to embrace our mortality with the awareness that we will make our passage to new life in solidarity with all the people of the earth.

A good death is a death in solidarity with others. To prepare ourselves for a good death, we must develop or deepen this sense of solidarity. If we live toward death as toward an event that separates us from people, death cannot be other than a sad and sorrowful event. But if we grow in awareness that our mortality, more than anything else, will lead us into solidarity with others, then death can become a celebration of our unity with the human race. Instead of separating us from others, death can unite us with others; instead of being sorrowful, it can give rise to new joy; instead of simply ending life, it can begin something new.

At first this might sound absurd. How can death create unity instead of separation? Isn't death the ultimate separation? It is, if we live by the norms of a competitive society always concerned with the question, Who is the strongest? But when we claim our divine childhood and learn to trust that we belonged to God before we were born and will belong to God after we have died, then we experience that all people on this planet are our brothers and sisters, and we are all making the journey together through birth and death to new life. We are not alone; beyond the differences that separate us, we share one common humanity and thus belong to each other. The mystery of life is that we discover this human together-ness not when we are powerful and strong, but when we are vulnerable and weak.

The experiential knowledge that we will all die can fill us with a profound joy and make it possible for us to face death freely and fearlessly. We can say not only, "It is good to live like everyone else," but also, "It is good to die like everyone else." Some of us die earlier, others later; some after a short life, others after a long life; some after an illness, others suddenly and unexpectedly. But all of us will die and participate in the same end. In light of this great human sameness, the many differences in how we live and die no longer have to separate us but can, to the contrary, deepen our sense of communion with one another. This communion with the whole human family, this profound sense of belonging to each other, takes the sting out of dying and points us far beyond the limits of our chronology.

Somehow, we know that our bond with one another is stronger than death.

We touch here the core of Jesus' message. Jesus didn't come to simply point us away from this world by promising a new life after death. He came to make us aware that, as children of his God, we are all his brothers and sisters, all brothers and sisters of each other; we can, therefore, live our lives together without fear of death. He wants us not only to participate in his divine childhood, but also to enjoy fully the brotherhood and sisterhood that emerges from this shared childhood. He says to us, "Just as the Father has loved me, so I have loved you" (John 15:9), and "You must love one another, just as I have loved you" (John 13:34).

The gospel writer John, writing many years after Jesus' death, clearly showed the intimate connection between our being children of God and our being brothers and sisters of one another. He said, "Let us love, then, because God loved us first. Anyone who says I love God and hates his brother or sister, is a liar, since whoever does not love the brother or sister that can be seen, cannot love God who cannot be seen. Indeed this is the commandment we have received, that whoever loves God, must also love his brother and sister" (1 John 4:19–21). The joy of this brotherhood and sisterhood allows us to die well, because we no longer have to die alone but can die in intimate solidarity with all people on this planet. This solidarity offers hope.

In a mysterious way, the people dying all over the world because of starvation, oppression, illness, despair, violence, and war become our teachers. In Somalia and Ethiopia, children are dying. As their brothers and sisters, we must help them live, but we also must understand that we will die as they do. In Bosnia, Muslims, Croats, and Serbs are dying. As their brothers and sisters, we must do everything to prevent them from killing each other, but we also must remain aware that we will die as they do. In Guatemala, Indians are dying. As their sisters and brothers, we must work hard to stop their oppressors in their murderous work, but we also must face the fact that we will die as they do. In many countries, young and old people are dying of cancer and AIDS. As their brothers and sisters, we must care for them as well as we can and keep looking for cures, but we should never forget that we will die as they do. Countless men and women are dying through poverty and neglect. As their brothers and sisters, we must offer them our resources and support. But we must remind ourselves continually that we will die as they do.

In their immense pain and grief, these people ask for solidarity, not only in life, but in death as well. Only when we are willing to let their dying help us to die well will we be able to help them to live well. When we can face death with hope, we can live life with generosity.

We all die poor. When we come to our final hours, nothing can help us survive. No amount of money, power, or influence can keep us from dying. This is true poverty. But Jesus said, "Blessed are you who are poor; the kingdom of God is yours" (Luke 6:20). There is a blessing hidden in the poverty of dying. It is the blessing that makes us brothers and sisters in the same Kingdom. It is the blessing we receive from others who die. It is the blessing we give to others when our time to die has come. It is the blessing that comes from the God whose life is everlasting. It is the blessing that reaches far beyond our birth and death. It is the blessing that carries us safely from eternity to eternity.

A friend who was very ill had a great devotion to Mary, the mother of Jesus, and decided to make a pilgrimage to Lourdes, France, to ask for healing. When she left, I was afraid that she would be disillusioned if no miracle happened. But on her return, she said, "Never did I see so many sick people. When I came face-to-face with that human suffering, I no longer wanted a miracle. I no longer wanted to be the exception. I experienced a deep desire to be one of them, to belong to these wounded people. Instead of praying for a cure, I prayed that I would have the grace to bear my illness in solidarity with them. And I trust that the mother of Jesus will bring my prayer to her Son."

I was deeply moved by this radical change in my friend's prayers. She who had hoped to be different from all those who are ill now wanted to be like them and to live her pain as their sister in suffering.

This story reveals the healing power of the experience of human solidarity. This healing power helps us not only to live our illness well, but also to die well. Indeed, we can be healed from our fear of death, not by a miraculous event that prevents us from dying, but by the healing experience of being a brother or sister of all humans—past, present, and future—who share with us the fragility of our existence. In this experience, we can taste the joy of being human and foretaste our communion with all people.

CHAPTER THREE

We Are Parents of Generations to Come

MARINA, my sister-in-law, is only forty-eight years old. She is dying. Five years ago, her doctor told her that she has cancer. Ever since, her life has been a long, painful attempt to fight the illness and to survive the many medical interventions. With three major surgeries and much chemotherapy, medical experts tried to remove the cancer and to prolong Marina's life.

My brother Paul did everything possible to offer his wife hope that there was a chance to beat the enemy. But finally he realized, as others with him realized, that the battle was lost. As I write this, Marina is preparing herself for death.

During the last few years, I have often had the opportunity to talk with Marina about her illness and even about her death. Marina is a strong, unsentimental woman. She likes to look at things as they are and has no time for people who try to comfort or console her with white lies. Although she has cooperated fully with the doctors and nurses who have helped her to fight her cancer, she does not want anyone to make any decision of which she is not fully a part. Nor does she want any spiritual support based on religious convictions that she does not hold. She often questions my spiritual viewpoints and has strong opinions about life and death — her own death as well as the deaths of others.

As the years go by and Marina's illness gets worse, she has expressed herself more and more through painting and poetry. These activities started as hobbies but have gradually become her primary activity. The weaker she has become physically, the stronger, more direct, and less adorned her artistic style has become. Her poems especially are the direct fruit of her struggle to befriend death.

Marina has lived an active and productive life. As a teacher and codirector of a language school, she built a career for herself and introduced creative new educational methods. But her illness has cruelly interrupted all of that and forced her to let go of the world she loved so much. Since her illness began, her art has replaced her many educational activities and become a new source of life for her. Often, when I am with her, she recites her poems by heart and asks me what I think of them. Many of them are playful and written with a humorous twist, but all express her increasing awareness that each day she has something more to let go of and that she is entering a time of many farewells.

As I have seen Marina prepare herself for her death, I have gradually realized that she is making her own dying a gift for others—not only for my brother Paul, not only for her family and friends, but also for the nurses and doctors and the many circles of people with whom she has spoken and shared her poems. Having taught all her life, she now teaches through her preparation for death. It strikes me that her successes and accomplishments will probably soon be forgotten, but the fruits of her dying may well last a long time. Marina is childless and has often wondered what her unique contribution to our society could be. Not having had the joy of motherhood, she has become the parent of many through the way she lives toward her death. The last five years might well prove to belong to the most fruitful of her life. She has shown me, in a whole new way, what it means to die for others. It means to become the parent of future generations.

Few of Jesus' words have affected me personally so much as his words about his own approaching death. With great directness, Jesus spoke to his closest friends about the end. Although he acknowledged the sorrow and sadness it would bring, he continued to announce his death as something good, something full of blessing, full of promise, full of hope. Shortly before his death, he said, "Now I am going to the one who sent me. No one of you asks, 'Where are you going?' Yet you are sad at heart because I have told you this. Still, I am telling you the truth: it is for your own good that I am going, because unless I go, the Spirit will not come to you; but if I go, I will send him to you. . . . I shall have many things to say to you but they would be too much for you to bear now. However, when the Spirit of truth comes he will lead you to the complete truth, since he will not be speaking of his own accord, but will say only what he has been told; and he will reveal to you the things to come" (John 16:4–7, 13).

At first, these words may sound strange, unfamiliar, even far away from our daily struggle with life and death. But after my conversations with Marina and with many other friends facing death, Jesus' words strike me in a new way and express the deepest significance of what these people are experiencing. We may be inclined to view the way Jesus prepared himself and his friends for his death as unique, far beyond any "normal" human way. But in fact, Jesus' way of dying offers us a hopeful example. We, too, can say to our friends,

"It is for your own good that I am going, because if I go I can send the Spirit to you, and the Spirit will reveal to you the things to come." Isn't this what Marina wants to say when she makes poems and paintings that will give new life to those who will mourn her death? Isn't "sending the Spirit" the best expression for not leaving those you love alone but offering them a new bond, deeper than the bond that existed in life? Doesn't "dying for others" mean dying so that others can continue to live, strengthened by the Spirit of our love?

Some people might protest, saying, "Jesus, the only Son of the Father, did send his Holy Spirit to us . . . but we are not Jesus, and we have no Holy Spirit to send!" But when we listen deeply to Jesus' words, we realize that we are called to live like him, to die like him, and to rise like him, because the Spirit—the Divine Love, which makes Jesus one with his Father—has been given to us. Not only the death of Jesus, but our death, too, is destined to be good for others. Not only the death of Jesus, but our death, too, is meant to bear fruit in other people's lives. Not only the death of Jesus, but our death, too, will bring the Spirit of God to those we leave behind. The great mystery is that all people who have lived with and in the Spirit of God participate through their deaths in the sending of the Spirit. Thus God's Spirit of love continues to be sent to us, and Jesus' death continues to bear fruit through all whose death is like his death, a death for others.

In this way, dying becomes the way to everlasting fruitfulness. Here is the most hope-giving aspect of death. Our death may be the end of our success, our productivity, our fame, or our importance among people, but it is not the end of our fruitfulness. In fact, the opposite is true: the fruitfulness of our lives shows itself in its fullness only after we have died. We ourselves seldom see or experience our own fruitfulness. Often we remain preoccupied with our accomplishments and have no eye for the fruitfulness of what we live. But the beauty of life is that it bears fruit long after life itself has come to an end. Jesus said, "In all truth I tell you, unless a wheat grain falls into the earth and dies, it remains only a single grain; but if it dies it yields a rich harvest" (John 12:24).

This is the mystery of Jesus' death and of the deaths of all who have lived in his Spirit. Their lives yield fruit far beyond the limits of their short and often localized existence. Years after my mother's death, she continues to bear fruit in my life. I am deeply aware that many of my major decisions since her death have been guided by the Spirit of Jesus, which she continues to send me.

Jesus lived less than forty years; he didn't travel outside his own country; the people who knew him during his life scarcely understood him; and when he died, only a few of his followers remained faithful. In every respect, his life was a failure. Success had left him, popularity had dwindled, and all his power was gone. Still, few lives have been so fruitful; few lives have affected the thinking and feeling of other people so deeply; few have so profoundly shaped future cultures; few have influenced so radically the patterns of human relationships. Jesus himself referred constantly to the fruitfulness of his life that would only become manifest after his death. Often he stressed that his disciples did not comprehend what he said or did, but that one day they would understand. When Jesus washed Peter's feet, he said, "At the moment you do not know what I am doing, but later you will understand" (John 13:7). When Jesus spoke about his return to the Father, he said, "I have said these things to you while still with you, but . . . the holy Spirit whom the Father will send in my name, will teach you everything and remind you of all that I have said to you" (John 14:25–26). The full meaning of Jesus' life was only revealed after his death.

Isn't this also true of many of the great men and women in history? For many of them, the full meaning of their lives became clear long after they died. Some were barely known during their lives, and some were known for completely different things than the things they are remembered for today. Some were successful and famous; others suffered from endless failures and rejections. But all truly great men and women who have shaped our ways of thinking and acting have borne fruit that they themselves couldn't see or predict.

Brother Lawrence is only one of many examples of this. This simple lay brother lived as a cook and shoemaker in a French Carmelite house of studies from 1614 to 1691. After his death, his letters and reflections about "walking in the presence of God" were made public, and even today they continue to affect the spiritual lives of many people. The life of Brother Lawrence was unspectacular but fruitful. Lawrence himself never thought much about influencing other people's lives. His only wish was to do all that he did in the presence of God.

The real question before our death, then, is not, How much can I still accomplish, or How much influence can I still exert? but, How can I live so that I can continue to be fruitful when I am no longer here among my family and friends? That question shifts our attention from doing to being. Our doing brings success, but our being bears fruit. The great paradox of our lives is that we are often concerned about what we do or still can do, but we are most likely to be remembered for who we were. If the Spirit guides our lives—the

Spirit of love, joy, peace, gentleness, forgiveness, courage, perseverance, hope, and faith—then that Spirit will not die but will continue to grow from generation to generation.

In pondering Marina's death and my own, I realize the great challenge of life. While the society in which I live keeps asking for the tangible results of my life, I must gradually learn to trust that those results may or may not prove to be significant. What really counts are the fruits that my life bears. As I grow older and weaker, I will be able to do less and less. Both my body and my mind will become weaker. My eyes will move closer to the book I want to read and my ears closer to the neighbor I am trying to understand. My failing memory will lead me to repeat my jokes more often, and my decreasing ability to reflect critically will turn me into a less interesting conversationalist. Nonetheless, I trust that God's Spirit will manifest itself in my weakness and move where it wants and bear fruit from my deteriorating body and mind.

So my death will indeed be a rebirth. Something new will come to be, something about which I cannot say or think much. It lies beyond my own chronology. It is something that will last and carry on from generation to generation. In this way, I become a new parent, a parent of the future.

I think of my friends with AIDS every day. Some of these people I know personally; some I know as friends of friends; many I know by what is written by them or about them. From the outset of this horrendous epidemic, I have felt close to the many young men and women who live with AIDS. They all know that they cannot live long and that they will die difficult and often painful deaths. I want so much to help them, to be with them, to console and comfort them. I am overwhelmed by the tragedy that, in their desperate desire to be embraced and cared for, many have found illness and death instead. I cry out to heaven, saying, "Why, O God, does the human search for communion and intimacy lead to separation and anguish? Why are so many young people who simply want to be loved languishing in hospitals and lonely rooms? Why are love and death so close to each other?" Maybe the why is not what is important. Important are the men and women with their beautiful names and beautiful faces who wonder why they didn't find the love they yearned for. I feel close to these people because their pain is not far from mine.

I, too, want to love and be loved. I, too, must die. I, too, know that mysterious connection between my heart's yearning for love and my heart's anguish. In my heart, I want to embrace and hold all these people who are dying—hungry for love.

Recently I read Paul Monette's deeply moving book *Borrowed Time*. In it, he describes in pain-filled detail his battle against the AIDS of his friend Roger Horwitz. The whole book is like one battle cry: "We will beat the enemy. We will not let this evil force destroy our lives." It is a heroic battle, in which every means of survival is tried. But it is a lost battle. Roger dies, and Paul remains alone. Is death finally stronger than love? Are we finally all losers? Is all our struggle to survive, in the end, a silly struggle, as silly as the struggle of a fox attempting to gnaw its way out of a leg trap?

Many must feel that way. Only their deep, human self-respect in the face of the unbeatable power of death makes them put up an honest fight. I admire strongly the way Paul and Roger fought their grim battle. But after a life of reflection on the death of Jesus and many of his followers, I want to believe that beyond the fatal battle for survival is a hopeful battle for life. I want to believe — indeed, I do believe — that, ultimately, love is stronger than death. I have no argument to present. I have only the story of Jesus and the stories of those who trust in the life-giving truth of his life and his word. These stories show me a new way of living and a new way of dying, and I have a profound desire to show that way to others.

When I visited Rick in Bethany House — the Catholic worker house for people with AIDS in Oakland,

California—I wanted to say something to him that Paul hadn't been able to say to Roger. In Paul's experience, the churches had nothing significant to say to people with AIDS. He could only think of churches as hypocritical, oppressive, and rejecting. He found more comfort in Greek mythology than in the Christian story. But when I held Rick's hand and looked into his fear-filled eyes, I felt deeply that the short time he had still to live could be more than a brave but losing battle for survival. I wanted him to know and believe that the meaning of the time left lay not in what he could still do but in the fruits he could bear when there was nothing left to do. When we were together, Rick said, "My friends shall have a future. I have only death to wait for." I didn't know what to say, and I knew that a lot of words wouldn't do him much good. Instead, I took his hand in mine and laid my other hand on his forehead. I looked into his tearful eyes and said, "Rick, don't be afraid. Don't be afraid. God is close to you, much closer than I am. Please trust that the time ahead of you will be the most important time of your life, not just for you, but for all of us whom you love and who love you." As I said these words, I felt Rick's body relax, and a smile came through his tears. He said, "Thank you, thank you." Then he reached out his arms and pulled me close to him and whispered in my ear, "I want to believe you. I really do, but it is so hard."

As I think of Rick and the many young people who are dying like him, everything in me rises in protest. I know that it is a temptation to think of people with AIDS as fighting a losing battle. But with all the faith I can muster, I believe that their deaths will be fruitful and that they are indeed called to be the parents of generations to come.

The Choice to Die Well

TO BEFRIEND DEATH, we must claim that we are
children of God, sisters and brothers of all people, and
parents of generations yet to come. In so doing, we
liberate our death from its absurdity and make it the
gateway to a new life.

In our society, in which childhood is something
to grow away from, in which wars and ethnic conflicts
constantly mock brotherhood and sisterhood among
people, and in which the greatest emphasis is on suc-
ceeding in the few years we have, it hardly seems possible that death could be a gateway to anything.

Still, Jesus has opened this way for us. When we
choose his way to live and die, we can face our death
with the mocking question of the apostle Paul: "Death,
where is your victory? Death, where is your sting?"
(1 Corinthians 15:55). This is a choice, but a hard
choice. The powers of darkness that surround us are

strong and easily tempt us to let our fear of death rule our thoughts, words, and actions.

But we *can choose* to befriend our death as Jesus did. We *can choose* to live as God's beloved children in solidarity with all people, trusting in our ultimate fruitfulness. And in so doing, we can also become people who care for others. As men and women who have faced our mortality, we can help our brothers and sisters to dispel the darkness of death and guide them toward the light of God's grace.

Let us turn now to the subject of care.

PART TWO

—

CARING WELL

At the Heart of Being Human

BEFRIENDING OUR DEATH is a lifelong spiritual task but a task that, in all its different nuances, deeply affects our relationships with our fellow human beings. Every step we take toward deeper self-understanding brings us closer to those with whom we share our lives. As we learn, over time, to live the truth that death does not have a sting, we find within ourselves the gift to guide others to discover the same truth. We do not first do one of these things and later the other. Befriending our own death and helping others to befriend theirs are inseparable. In the realm of the Spirit of God, living and caring are one.

Our society suggests that caring and living are quite separate and that caring belongs primarily to professionals who have received special training. Although training *is* important, and although certain people need preparation to practice their profession with competence, caring is the privilege of every person and is at the heart of being human. When we look at the original meaning of the word *profession* and realize that the term refers, first of all, to professing one's own deepest conviction, then the essential spiritual unity between living and caring becomes clear.

In the following three chapters, I reflect on caring for the dying. First, I look at caring for the dying as helping our fellow human beings to befriend their own deaths. In these reflections, I hope to make clear that, to the degree that we befriend our own death, we can become truly caring people. Paralleling the first three chapters of this book, I look at care as helping others to claim for themselves the spiritual truth that they are—as we are—children of God, brothers and sisters of each other, and parents of generations to come.

CHAPTER FOUR

You Are a Child of God

MAURICE GOULD, who died ten days before I began writing this book, was one of the first people I met at Daybreak. He was a member of the "Green House," the house where I spent my first week. Moe was born with Down's syndrome. For many years, he lived with his parents and sister, who cared for him lovingly. When he was in his early forties, he came to Daybreak. Two years ago, Maurice began to show signs of Alzheimer's disease. From then until his death, the community tried to care for him in the special way that Alzheimer patients require. The doctors told us that Moe would not be able to live long and that we must prepare him, as well as ourselves, for his death.

For those who were close to Moe—his family, his friends, and those who lived with him in the Green

House—caring for him became a great challenge, a challenge at once painful and joyful. As Moe gradually lost his memory, his ability to recognize people, his sense of orientation, and his ability to feed himself, he became increasingly anxious and could no longer be his old good-humored self. Seeing him slip into a state of complete dependence, needing more help than we could offer him, was difficult. Finally Moe was taken to the nearby hospital, where a competent staff, together with the members of the Green House, cared for him during the last months of his life.

Among the things I remember most about Moe are his generous hugs. Often he would walk up to me with both hands stretched out and ready for a big embrace. As he held me, he would whisper in my ear, "Amazing Grace," his cue for me to sing his favorite song with him. I also remember his love for dancing, his love of food, and his love for making people laugh with his imitations. When he imitated me, he put his glasses upside down on his nose and made wild gestures.

As I sit in Freiburg, far away from my community, and think of Moe, I realize more than ever that Moe was, and became evermore, a child of God. Because his friends were allowed to be so close to his "second childhood," they were able to care for him with great patience and lavish generosity.

Moe's illnesses—Down's syndrome and Alzheimer's disease—showed in a dramatic way the journey we all must make somewhere, somehow. But at the end of that journey, what do we finally see? Do we see a person who has lost all human abilities and has become a burden for everyone, or do we see a person who has become evermore a child of God, a pure instrument of grace? I cannot help but think about the countless times Moe looked me in the eyes and said, "Amazing Grace." I was not always ready to sing the old song again, and often I would say, "Next time, Moe." Now that Moe is gone, I keep hearing his persistent words—"Amazing Grace, Amazing Grace"—God's way of announcing to me the mystery of Moe's life and of all people.

Many of the people in Daybreak cannot do what most people outside the community can do. Some cannot walk, some cannot speak, some cannot feed themselves, some cannot read, some cannot count, some cannot dress themselves, and a few can do none of these things. No one is waiting for a cure. We only know that things will get harder as we get older and that the difference between people with a disability and those without a disability will become ever smaller. What are we ultimately growing toward? Are we simply becoming less capable people, returning our bodies to the dust from which they came, or are we growing into living reminders of that amazing grace that Moe always wanted to sing about?

We must choose between these two radically different viewpoints. The choice to see our own and other people's decreasing abilities as gateways to God's grace is a choice of faith. It is a choice based on the conviction that we see not only failure on the cross of Jesus but victory as well, not only destruction but new life as well, not only nakedness but glory as well. When John, the beloved disciple, looked up to Jesus and saw blood and water flowing from Jesus' pierced side, he saw something other than proof that all was over. He saw fulfillment of the prophecy "They will look up to the one whom they have pierced," a glimpse of God's victory over death, and a sign of God's amazing grace. John wrote, "This is evidence of the one who saw it—true evidence, and he knows that what he says is true—and he gives it so that you may believe as well" (John 19:35).

That is the choice of faith. It is the choice we make when we say that Moe, with his body and mind completely depleted by Alzheimer's disease, brought to us, through his dying and death, an amazing grace. It's the choice we make when we care for dying people with all the tenderness and gentleness that God's beloved children deserve. It's the choice that allows us to see the face of Jesus in the poor, the addicted, and those who live with AIDS and cancer. It's the choice of the human heart that has been touched by the Spirit of Jesus and is able to recognize that Spirit wherever people are dying.

Recently I attended a meeting of the leaders of several Christian institutions responsible for the supervision of homes for people with mental disabilities. In our free-market economy, they told me, human care is spoken of in terms of supply and demand. In this context, the suffering person becomes the buyer of care, and the care professional becomes the merchant of care. It seems to me that this language and the vision that underlies it reduce the human person to nothing but a commodity in the competitive world of high finance. In this language, a vision has been chosen that no longer encourages us to celebrate the dying and the death of people like Maurice Gould. Amazing grace has been replaced by not-so-amazing business considerations.

Care, as I speak of it here, is the loving attention given to another person—not because that person needs it to stay alive, not because that person or some insurance company is paying for it, not because care provides jobs, not because the law forbids our hastening death, and not because that person can be used for medical research, but because that person is a child of God, just as we are.

To care for others as they become weaker and closer to death is to allow them to fulfill their deepest vocation, that of becoming ever-more fully what they already are: daughters and sons of God. It is to help them to claim, especially in their dying hours, their divine childhood and to let the Spirit of God cry out from their hearts, "Abba, Father" (Galatians 4:9). To care for the dying is to keep saying, "You are the beloved daughter of God, you are the beloved son of God."

How do we say this? The ways are countless: through words, prayers, and blessings; through gentle touch and the holding of hands; through cleaning and feeding; through listening and just being there. Some of these forms of care may be helpful, some not. But all are ways of expressing our faith that those we care for are precious in God's eyes. Through our caring presence, we keep announcing that sacred truth: dying is not a sweet, sentimental event; it is a great struggle to surrender our lives completely. This surrender is not an obvious human response. To the contrary: we want to cling to whatever is left. It is for this reason that dying people have so much anguish. As did Jesus, dying people too often experience their total powerlessness as rejection and abandonment. Often the agonizing cry "My God, my God, why have you abandoned me?" (Matthew 27:47) makes it difficult to say, "Father into your hands I commend my Spirit" (Luke 23:46).

Moe was not spared this struggle. As Alzheimer's disease took away his already-limited abilities to direct his own life, a great anguish grew within him. He often cried out in agony, and he experienced an ever-growing fear of aloneness. Often, during the night, he wanted to get up and go to work. Among the last words he could say were, "Call me . . . call me . . . call me."

Moe's fear was no different from my own. It was the fear of being rejected or left alone; of being found a burden or a nuisance; of being laughed at or considered useless. It was the deep fear of not belonging, of excommunication, of final abandonment. The more intimately I come to know people with mental disabilities, the more I am convinced that their deepest suffering is not in their inability to read, study, speak, or walk but in their deep fear of rejection, of being a burden; in this respect, they do not differ from me. Our greatest suffering comes from losing touch with my/our belovedness and thinking of ourselves only as a useless, unwanted presence.

Caring for others is, first of all, helping them to overcome that enormous temptation of self-rejection. Whether we are rich or poor, famous or unknown, disabled or fully abled, we all share the fear of being left alone and abandoned, a fear that remains hidden under the surface of our self-composure. It is rooted much more deeply than in the possibility of not being liked or loved by people. Its deepest root lies in the possibility of not being loved at all, of not belonging to anything that lasts, of being swallowed up by a dark nothingness—yes, of being abandoned by God.

Caring, therefore, is being present to people as they fight this ultimate battle, a battle that becomes evermore real and intense as death approaches. Dying and death always call forth, with renewed power, the fear that we are unloved and will, finally, be reduced to useless ashes. To care is to stand by a dying person and to be a living reminder that the person is indeed the beloved child of God.

Mary's standing under the cross is the most moving expression of that care. Her son died in agony. She was there: not speaking, not pleading, not crying. She was there, reminding her son by her silent presence that, while she could not keep him for herself, his true sonship belongs to the Father, who will never leave him alone. She helped him recall his own words: "The time will come . . . when you will leave me alone. And yet I am not alone, because the Father is with me" (John 16:32). Mary encouraged Jesus to move beyond his experience of abandonment and to surrender himself into the embrace of his Father. She was there to strengthen his faith that, even in the midst of darkness, where he can feel nothing but loss and rejection, he remains the beloved Son of God, who will never leave him alone. It was this motherly care that finally allowed Jesus to win the battle against the demonic powers of rejection, to ward off the temptation of abandonment, and to surrender his whole being to God, with the words, "Father into your hands I commend my Spirit" (Luke 23:46).

Can we care as Mary did? I don't believe we can care in this way on our own. Even Mary was not alone. John, the beloved disciple, was with her beneath the cross. Reminding people in their agony of their divine childhood is not something we can do on our own. The powers of darkness are strong, and we can easily be pulled into the darkness ourselves and drawn into enormous self-doubts. To stand by a person who is dying is to participate in the immense struggle of faith. It is a struggle no person should take on alone. Before we realize it, the anguish of our dying friend becomes ours, and we become the victim of the same powers our friend is struggling with. We become overwhelmed by feelings of helplessness, powerlessness, self-doubt, and even guilt linked to our often-unacknowledged wish that it all would end soon.

No, we shouldn't try to care by ourselves. Care is not an endurance test. We should, whenever possible, care together with others. It is the community of care that reminds the dying person of his or her belovedness. It is Mary *and* John, Lori *and* Carl, Loretta *and* David, Carol *and* Peter, Janice *and* Cheryl, Geoff *and* Carrie, Lorenzo *and* many others who together can stand at the foot of the cross and say, "You are the beloved child of God, now as always." This circle of love surrounding our dying friends has the power to expel the demons of self-rejection and abandonment and bring light in the midst of darkness. I saw it happening around Moe, and I see it happening in the AIDS community and in the networks of support for cancer patients. Together, as a body of love, as a community that cares, we can come close to the dying and discover there a new hope, a new life, and a new strength to live. There can be smiles and stories, new encounters and new knowledge about ways to help, beautiful moments of silence and prayer. There can be the gift of people being together, waiting patiently for death to come. Together we can create that place where our dying friends can feel safe and can gradually let go and make the passage knowing that they are loved.

Caring together is the basis of community life. We don't come together simply to console each other or even to support each other. Important as those things may be, long-term community life is directed in other ways. Together we reach out to others. Together we look at those who need our care. Together we carry our suffering brothers and sisters to the place of rest, healing, and safety.

I have always been impressed with the thought that people are only ready to commit themselves to each other when they no longer focus on each other but rather focus together on the larger world beyond themselves. Falling in love makes us look at each other with admiration and tenderness. Committing ourselves to one another in love makes us look together toward those who need our care: the child, the stranger, the poor, the dying. That commitment lies at the heart of every community.

When I reflect on my own community, the L'Arche Daybreak community in Toronto, I realize increasingly that what keeps us faithful to each other is our common commitment to care for people with mental disabilities. We are called to care together. No one in our community could care single-handedly for any one of our disabled members. Not only would it be physically impossible, but it would quickly lead to emotional and mental exhaustion. Together, however, we can create a caring space that is good, not only for those who receive care, but also for those who give it. In this space, the boundaries between receiving and giving vanish, and true community can start to exist. It is essential to the weakest members of our community that those who care for them do so together. These members say to us, "For me to live, you must love not just me, but each other, too."

When I reflect on community life through the ages, I can easily see how the "ups" are closely connected to the vibrancy of caring together and the "downs" to absorption in internal matters. Even the most contemplative, seemingly hidden community could stay alive and well only when its life remained a life reaching out beyond the boundaries of the community. Even a life dedicated to prayer and meditation needs to maintain a quality of caring together for others. The mystery of this caring together is that it not only asks for community, but also creates it.

Those who cared for Moe realized after his death that he had brought them closer than they were before. Just as the dying Jesus brought Mary and John closer to each other by giving them to each other as mother and son, so too did Moe bring his friends closer to each other as sons and daughters of the same God. All true care for the dying person brings new awareness of the bonds that create a community of love.

The Flying Rodleighs are trapeze artists who perform in the German circus Simoneit-Barum. When the circus came to Freiburg two years ago, my friends Franz and Reny invited me and my father to see the show. I will never forget how enraptured I became when I first saw the Rodleighs move through the air, flying and catching as elegant dancers. The next day, I returned to the circus to see them again and introduced myself to them as one of their great fans. They invited me to attend their practice sessions, gave me free tickets, asked me to dinner, and suggested I travel with them for a week in the near future. I did, and we became good friends.

One day, I was sitting with Rodleigh, the leader of the troupe, in his caravan, talking about flying. He said, "As a flyer, I must have complete trust in my catcher. The public might think that I am the great star of the trapeze, but the real star is Joe, my catcher. He has to be there for me with split-second precision and grab me out of the air as I come to him in the long jump." "How does it work?" I asked. "The secret," Rodleigh said, "is that the flyer does nothing and the catcher does everything. When I fly to Joe, I have simply to stretch out my arms and hands and wait for him to catch me and pull me safely over the apron behind the catchbar."

"You do nothing!" I said, surprised. "Nothing," Rodleigh repeated. "The worst thing the flyer can do is to try to catch the catcher. I am not supposed to catch Joe. It's Joe's task to catch me. If I grabbed Joe's wrists, I might break them, or he might break mine, and that would be the end for both of us. A flyer must fly, and a catcher must catch, and the flyer must trust, with outstretched arms, that his catcher will be there for him."

When Rodleigh said this with so much conviction, the words of Jesus flashed through my mind: "Father into your hands I commend my Spirit." Dying is trusting in the catcher. To care for the dying is to say, "Don't be afraid. Remember that you are the beloved child of God. He will be there when you make your long jump. Don't try to grab him; he will grab you. Just stretch out your arms and hands and trust, trust, trust."

CHAPTER FIVE

You Are Brothers and Sisters of Each Other

ONE DAY, Sally, a good friend of mine, said, "It has been five years since my husband, Bob, died, and I would like to visit his grave with my children. Would you be willing to come with us?" When I said, "Of course, I would love to come with you," she told me what had happened. Bob had died unexpectedly from heart failure, and Sally had suddenly been faced with the hard task of helping her children, Mitchell and Lindsay, who were four and five at the time, to respond to their father's death. She had felt then that it would be too difficult for the children to see their father being put into the ground and covered with sand. "They are much too young to understand," Sally had thought.

As the years went by, the cemetery became a fearful place for Sally, Lindsay, and Mitchell. Intuitively, Sally felt that something was not right. And so she invited me to go with her and the children to Bob's grave. It was still a little too scary for Lindsay, because she had such concrete memories of Bob, so only Mitchell came along.

It was a beautiful, sunny day. We soon found Bob's grave: a simple stone engraved with the words "A kind and gentle man." We sat on the grass around the stone, and Sally and Mitchell told stories about Bob. Mitchell remembered how his dad had played ball with him. When his memory became hazy, Sally filled in the details. I just asked questions.

As we began to feel more at ease, I said, "Wouldn't it be nice to have a picnic here? Maybe one day we could all come back, bring food and drinks with us, and celebrate Bob's life, right here at his grave. We could eat together in his memory." At first Sally and Mitchell were puzzled with the idea, but then Mitchell said, "Yes, why not? Then I am sure Lindsay will come, too."

When Sally and Mitchell went home, they told Lindsay that it hadn't been scary at all but had been quite all right. A few days later, Lindsay asked Sally to take her to the grave. They went and talked together about Bob. Gradually, Bob became less a stranger and more a new friend, and having a picnic on his grave became something to look forward to. After all, Jesus, too, had asked his friends to remember him with a meal.

This story shows how easily we distance ourselves from those who have died and treat them as fearful strangers who remind us of things we don't want to be reminded of—especially our own mortality. But it also shows how easily we can bring those who have died back into the circle of the living and make them gentle friends who can help us to face our own death.

How often do we see someone die? How often do we see a dead person? How often do we throw sand on top of a coffin that has been lowered into the grave? How often do we go to the cemetery and stand, kneel, or sit in front of the place where our spouse, parents, brothers, sisters, aunts, uncles, or friends have been buried? Are we still in touch with those who have died, or are we living our lives as if those who lived before us never really existed?

In Geysteren, the little village where my father lives in the southern part of Holland, the dead are still part of the daily life of the people. The cemetery, close to the village square, is a beautifully kept garden. The gate is freshly painted, the hedges well trimmed, the walkways raked clean, and each grave well cared for. Many of the memorial crosses or stones are decorated with fresh flowers or evergreen plants. The cemetery feels like a place where visitors are welcome and where it is good to spend time. The villagers love their cemetery. They go there, often, to pray and to be with their family or friends who have left them. During each service in the village church, "those who rest in [the] cemetery" are mentioned and included in the prayers of the community.

Whenever I visit my father in Geysteren, I go to that little cemetery. Close to the entrance, on the left side, is my mother's grave, marked with a simple brown wooden cross on which her name and the dates of her birth and death are painted in white. In front of the cross, evergreen plants outline the place where her body is laid to rest, and newly planted violets cover the center. When I stand before that simple grave, look at the cross, and hear the wind play with the leaves of the tall poplars surrounding the cemetery, I know that I am not alone. My mother is there, and she speaks to me. There is no apparition, no mysterious voice, but there is the simple, inner knowledge that she who died more than fourteen years ago is still with me. Embraced by the solitude of the beautiful cemetery, I hear her say that I must be faithful to my own journey and not be afraid to join her someday in death.

As I stand in front of my mother's grave, the circles of the dead surrounding me become ever wider. I am surrounded not only by the villagers who lie buried there, but also by family members and friends. Even wider is the circle of those whose actions and words have shaped my life and thoughts. Beyond are the many circles of the countless men and women whose names I do not know but who have, in their own unique way, made the journey that I am making and shared in the pains and joys of being human.

The poplars of the little cemetery in Geysteren sing their songs for all these people buried wide and far. Some were buried with the same gentleness as my mother was, some simply put away and forgotten, many dumped into mass graves of which few know the location and where no one ever comes to pray. For all of these people, the poplars sing, and standing in that cemetery, I feel grateful for being human as all of these people were and for being called to die as they did.

What a gift it is to know deeply that we are all brothers and sisters in one human family and that, different as our cultures, languages, religions, lifestyles, or work may be, we are all mortal beings called to surrender our lives into the hands of a loving God. What a gift it is to feel connected with the many who have died and to discover the joy and peace that flow from that connectedness. As I experience that gift, I know in a new way what it means to care for the dying. It means to connect them with the many who are dying or have died and to let them discover the intimate bonds that reach far beyond the boundaries of our short lives.

Going with Sally and Mitchell to Bob's grave and standing silently in the Geysteren cemetery in front of the place where my mother is buried have strengthened my conviction that all who are dying should know about the deep communion among all men and women on this planet. We human beings belong together, whether we live now or lived long ago, whether we live close by or far away, whether we have biological ties or not. We are brothers and sisters, and our dying is truly a dying in communion with each other.

But when we look at the world around us, the question arises: Do we really live as brothers and sisters? Every day, the newspapers and television remind us that human beings are fighting each other, torturing each other, killing each other. All over the world, people are the victims of persecution, war, and starvation. All over the world there is hatred, violence, and abuse. For a while, we lived with the illusion that the period of concentration camps was far behind us, that a holocaust such as that which occurred during the Second World War would no longer be humanly possible. But what is happening today shows how little we have really learned. The true sin of humanity is that men and women created to be brothers and sisters become again and again each other's enemies, willing to destroy each other's lives.

God sent Jesus to restore the true human order. Jesus is called the Redeemer. He came to redeem us from our sins and to remind us of the truth that we are sons and daughters of God, brothers and sisters of one another. How did Jesus redeem us from our sins? By becoming one of us: being born as we are born, living as we live, suffering as we suffer, and dying as we die. Indeed, Jesus became our brother, God-with-us. When the angel of God came to Nazareth and spoke to Joseph in a dream, he said, "Joseph, son of David, do not be afraid to take Mary home as your wife because she has conceived what is in her by the Holy Spirit. She will give birth to a son and you must name him Jesus, because he is the one who is to save his people from their sins." The evangelist Matthew, who wrote this, added, "Now all this took place to fulfill what the Lord had spoken through the prophet: 'Look! the virgin is with child and will give birth to a son whom they will call Immanuel,' a name which means 'God-with-us'" (Matthew 1:20–23).

God became God-with-us, our brother, so that we might claim for ourselves our brotherhood and sisterhood with all people. That is the story of Jesus, the story of our redemption. The heart of that story is that, in and through Jesus, God wanted to share not only our life, but our death. Jesus' death is the most radical expression of God's desire to be God-with-us. Nothing makes all human beings so similar to each other as their mortality. Our common mortality shows the illusion of our differences, the falseness of the many divisions among us, and the sins of our mutual enmities. By dying with and for us, Jesus wanted to dispel our illusions, heal our divisions, and forgive our sins so that we can rediscover that we are each other's brothers and sisters. By becoming our brother, Jesus wanted us to become once again brothers and sisters for one another. In nothing but sin did he want to differ from us. That is why he died for us. As one who was as mortal as we are, Jesus called us to stop living in fear of each other and to start loving one another. And this was more than his wish. It was his commandment, because it belongs to the essence of our being human. Jesus said, "This is my commandment, love one another as I have loved you. No one can have greater love than to lay down his life for his friends. You are my friends, if you do what I command you, . . . I shall no longer call you servants, because a servant does not know his master's business; I call you friends because I have made known to you everything that I have learned from my Father. . . . My command to you is to love one another" (John 15:12–17).

This great mystery of God becoming God-with-us has radical implications for the way we care for the dying. When God wants to die with and for us, we too must die with and for each other. Tragically, however, we think about our death first as an event that separates us from others. It is departing. It is leaving others behind. It is the ending of precious relationships, the beginning of loneliness. Indeed, for us, death is primarily a separation and, worse, an irreversible separation.

But Jesus died for us so that our death no longer need be just separation. His death opened for us the possibility of making our own death a way to union and communion. That's the radical turn that our faith allows us to make, but making that turn does not happen spontaneously. It requires care.

To care for the dying means to help them live their dying as a way to gather around them not only those who come to visit, not only family and friends, but all of humanity, the living as well as the dead. When we say that it is not good for a human being to die alone, we touch a deep mystery. In our death, we need to be, more than ever, in communion with others. The passage of our life is the passage that, more than any other passage, needs to be made with others.

There is something so obvious about this that no one would ever question the importance of being with someone at the moment of death. One of our worst fears about dying is that we might die without anyone at our side. We want someone to hold our hand, someone to touch us and speak gently to us, someone to pray with us. And that's what we want to do for others.

But there is more—much more—that is less obvious. To care also means to gently encourage our dying friend to die with and for others. Somehow, we who care need to have the courage to bring together around our dying friends the saints and sinners of all times: the starving children, the tortured prisoners, the homeless, the wanderers, the AIDS-afflicted, and the millions who have died or are now dying. At first, this might seem harsh, even cruel, but the opposite is true. It lifts our dying friends out of their isolation and makes them part of the most human of all human events. When those who are dying begin to realize that what they are experiencing, though painful, unites them with the worldwide and centuries-old family of humanity, they may be able to let go and gradually let that human family carry them through the gate of death.

For this reason, through the course of Christian history, dying people have been encouraged to look at the cross. On the famous sixteenth-century Isenheimer Altar in Colmar, France, Christ is portrayed hanging on the cross in unspeakable agony. His body is covered with sores caused by the black plague. When those who were dying of the plague looked up at that suffering Christ, they saw not only Jesus, who died with and for them long ago, but also all their dying brothers and sisters. There they found consolation. They realized that, as Christ had died for them, they too could die for their brothers and sisters and so make their dying an act of human solidarity.

Recently, in San Francisco, I saw a cross on which Jesus was dying of AIDS. There, too, all men, women, and children of the world with AIDS were portrayed, not to frighten, but to offer hope. The dying people of our century can look up to this cross and find hope.

Caring, then, is different from protecting dying people from seeing the larger picture. To the contrary, it is helping these people to grow in their awareness that their individual, painful condition is embedded in the basic condition of human mortality and, as such, can be lived in communion with others.

This care can be seen today in the many AIDS communities. In North American cities, young people are supporting each other as they live their illness in solidarity with each other and with others who are dying. They may seldom think or talk about this solidarity as an expression of God's solidarity with us, but even so, they do help each other to die in the same spirit in which Jesus died, the spirit of communion with the larger human family.

Is there anything practical to say about care for the dying in this perspective? Maybe only that dying people can face the reality of life much better than caregivers often realize. We have a tendency to keep the "bad news" of our world hidden from those who are dying. We want to offer these people a quiet, undisturbed, "peaceful" end. To accomplish that, we are inclined to avoid telling them about other people who are sick or dying, to avoid speaking with them about the victims of war and starvation in other places of the world. We want to keep them separated from the terrible realities of life. But do we offer them a service in doing so? Or do we prevent them from living their illness in solidarity with their fellow human beings and making their death a death with and for others?

Illness, and especially terminal illness, tends to narrow a person's vision, because people quickly become preoccupied with their own medical ups and downs and the daily events connected with their health. The often repeated question "How are you doing?" encourages people to tell and retell their own story, often against their desire.

I think many people desire to remain part of the larger world and would be glad to hear and speak about things outside their home or hospital. I remember vividly how grateful I was during my hospital stay after my accident for visitors who didn't ask or speak about me but rather focused my attention on something larger than myself. In fact, I felt grateful *not* to be separated from the world. I felt encouraged and strengthened by the assumption of my friends that my illness did not prevent me from being truly interested in the struggles of other people. Being connected and constantly reconnected with the larger suffering of my brothers and sisters in the human family did not paralyze me. To the contrary, this connection had a healing effect. Healing came not from being infantilized but from being treated as a mature adult able to live pain together with others.

I am not suggesting that we care for dying people simply by telling them about all the misery in the world. That would be unwise and unhelpful. I am not suggesting that we cause our dying friends to worry about the suffering of others. I *am* suggesting that, when we ourselves have befriended our own mortality, we will have no need to isolate our dying friends and will intuitively know how to maintain their communion with the larger, suffering human family. When we who care are not afraid to die, we will be better able to prepare the dying for death and deepen their communion with others instead of separating them.

A few years ago, the IMAX company made a short film, called *The Blue Planet*, from a space shuttle. The film is shown on a huge, concave screen with sounds coming from all sides. The viewers feel as if they are, in fact, sitting in the shuttle. The most remarkable part of this film is that it allows us to see what astronauts see: our own planet. For the first time in human history, we are able to see the earth from a distance. As we look at our earth, we realize that the beautiful blue ball moving through the universe is our own home. We can say, "Look! That's where we live, where we work, where we have our family. That's our home. Isn't it a beautiful place to live?"

As we look at that beautiful, majestic blue planet as our home, we suddenly have a completely new understanding of the word *our*. *Our* means all people, from all the continents, of all colors, religions, races, and ages. Seen from the space shuttle, the many differences among people that cause hatred, violence, war, oppression, starvation, and mutual destruction seem ridiculous. From the distance of the space shuttle, it is crystal clear that we have the same home, that we belong together, that together we must care for our beautiful blue planet so that we will be able to live here, not just now, but for the long future. Our space age has made it possible for us to grow into a new consciousness of the basic unity of all people on earth and the common responsibility of all people to care for each other and, together, for our home. Seeing our blue planet from a distance, we can say in a new way,

"We are indeed brothers and sisters, as Jesus told us long ago. We all are born as fragile beings; we all die as fragile beings. We need each other and our beautifully made home to live well and to die well."

The distant view of our home may make it possible for us to live and die with a deeper knowledge of being children of one God and brothers and sisters of each other and to truly care.

CHAPTER SIX

You Are Parents of Generations to Come

LAST YEAR, during Holy Week, while having dinner with some friends in downtown Toronto, I received a phone call that Connie Ellis, my secretary and close friend for the past six years, had suddenly become ill and been taken to the hospital. Until late that afternoon, she had tried hard to finish work on a text that I needed to take with me to Europe after Easter. She had gone home tired and suddenly had felt disoriented and anxious. Happily, she was still able to call her daughter-in-law, Carmen. When Carmen heard Connie's slurred and barely understandable speech, she became worried and hurried to see her at Connie's home.

Tests the next day showed that Connie had suffered a stroke caused by a large brain tumor. On Good

Friday, she underwent extensive surgery. Although the surgery was "successful," it left her paralyzed on her left side, unable to walk by herself, and in constant danger of falling. After extensive radiation therapy, doctors told Connie that the cancer was in remission. But she remained fragile, without much prospect that things would ever be "normal" for her again.

For years, Connie had been known for her great vitality, her competence, and her ability to accomplish a lot in a short time. She had become both my right and my left hand. She knew all the people who came to the office, phoned in, or wrote and had developed a warm relationship with many of them. The help, support, and advice she had given to countless people during the six years we worked together had made her a friend of many. Her ministry had become as important as my own.

Then, in an instant, all that was over. She who had always been eager to help others now needed others to help her. In one day, a strong, healthy, active, efficient woman had become fully dependent on family and friends. It was painful for me to see my close friend and co-worker suddenly lose her ability to do many things and help many people. But I was also hopeful in seeing that this radical change had not affected her trusting and loving disposition. Often Connie would say to me, "I feel deep inner peace. I am sure God will perform a miracle for me, but if not, I am ready to die. I have had a beautiful life."

As I reflect on this dramatic event in Connie's life and realize that she is, in fact, one of many people who have similar experiences, I wonder what meaning to give it. We human beings cannot live without meaning. Whatever happens to us, we ask, "Why is this happening to me? What does it mean?"

Much of the meaning in Connie's life has come from her relationships with her two sons, John and Steve, and their families. Her close friendships with Steve's wife, Carmen, and with her two grandchildren, Charles and Sarah, especially, have given her great joy and satisfaction. One of Connie's joys before her illness was to take Charles to play hockey and to encourage him from the sidelines. I could be critical about anyone else in Connie's presence, but not about "Carm and the kids," who were simply beyond criticism.

Much meaning also has come from Connie's work in the office. To the last minute of her working life, she enjoyed immensely what she was doing and did it with a never-abating dedication. I remember how happy she was that she had been able to transcribe all my interviews with the five trapeze artists in the circus. She fervently supported me in my "crazy" idea to write a book about them and wanted to be sure that I had all the necessary texts before returning to Germany for more interviews. Our work together, in all its variety and hecticness, gave meaning to her life. Few people realized that she was already past seventy and getting tired at times.

When, suddenly, everything changed, the question of meaning returned in full force. For a while, the emphasis was on getting better and being independent again. "Once I can drive my car again," Connie would say, "I won't be so dependent on John, Steve, Carm, and the kids anymore and will be able to manage by myself again." But she gradually came to see that this might never be possible. For the rest of her life, she might need others to help her.

To care for Connie and for the many who can no longer expect to return to their work, who can no longer be of service to their families and friends, is to search together for new meaning, a meaning no longer drawn from activities to get things done. Somehow, meaning must grow out of the "passivities" of waiting.

Jesus moved in his life from action to passion. For several years, he was extremely active preaching, teaching, and helping, always surrounded by large crowds and always moving from place to place. But in the Garden of Gethsemane, after his last supper with his disciples, he was handed over to those who resented him and his words. He was handed over to be the object of actions by others. From that moment, Jesus no longer took initiatives. He no longer did anything. Everything was done to him. He was arrested, put in prison, ridiculed, tortured, condemned, and crucified. All action was gone. The mystery of Jesus' life is that he fulfilled his vocation not through action but through becoming the subject of other people's actions. When he finally said, "It is fulfilled" (John 19:30), he meant not only "All I needed to do I have done," but also "All that needed to be done to me has been done to me." Jesus completed his mission on earth through being the passive subject of what others did to him.

What Jesus lived we also are called to live. Our lives, when lived in the spirit of Jesus, will find their fulfillment in a similar kind of dependence. Jesus made this clear when he said to Peter, "When you were young, you put on your belt and walked where you liked, but when you grow old, you will stretch out your hands and somebody else will put a belt round you and take you where you rather would not go" (John 21:18). We, too, must move from action to "passion," from being in control to being dependent, from taking initiatives to having to wait, from living to dying.

Painful and nearly impossible as this move seems to be, it is in this movement that our true fruitfulness is hidden. Our years of action are years of success and accomplishment. During these years, we do things about which we can speak with pride. But much of this success and many of these accomplishments will soon lie behind us. We might still point to them in the form of trophies, medals, or artistic products. But what is beyond our success and productivity? Fruitfulness lies beyond and that fruitfulness comes through passion, or suffering. Just as the ground can only bear fruit if broken by the plow, our own lives can only be fruitful if opened through passion. Suffering is precisely "undergoing" action by others, over which we have no control. Dying is always suffering, because dying always puts us in the place where others do to us whatever they decide to do, good or bad.

It is not easy to trust that our lives will bear fruit through this sort of dependence because, for the most part, we ourselves experience dependence as uselessness and as burdensome. We often feel discomfort, fatigue, confusion, disorientation, and pain, and it is hard to see any fruit coming from such vulnerability. We see only a body and a mind broken to pieces by the plow that others hold in their hands.

Believing that our lives come to fulfillment in dependence requires a tremendous leap of faith. Everything that we see or feel and everything that our society suggests to us through the values and ideas it holds up to us point in the opposite direction. Success counts, not fruitfulness—and certainly not fruitfulness that comes through passivity. But passion is God's way, shown to us through the cross of Jesus. It's the way we try to avoid at all costs, but it is the way to salvation. This explains why it is so important to care for the dying. To care for the dying is to help the dying make that hard move from action to passion, from success to fruitfulness, from wondering how much they can still accomplish to making their very lives a gift for others. Caring for the dying means helping the dying discover that, in their increasing weakness, God's strength becomes visible.

The well-known words of the apostle Paul, "God chose those who by human standards are weak to shame the strong" (1 Corinthians 1:27), take on new meaning here because the weak are not only the poor, the disabled, and the mentally ill, but also the dying—and all of us will be dying one day. We must trust that it is also in *this* weakness that God shames the strong and reveals true human fruitfulness. That's the mystery of the cross. When Jesus was on the cross, his life became infinitely fruitful. There, the greatest weakness and the greatest strength met. We can participate in this mystery through our death. To help each other die well is to help each other claim the fruitfulness in our weakness. Thus our dying enables us to embrace our cross with the trust that new life will emerge. Much of this becomes concrete when we are with people who must come to terms with their approaching death.

After her brain surgery, Connie always expressed a double desire: the desire for "a miracle," as she called it—to be completely cured and to be able to resume a normal life—and the desire to die peacefully, without causing too much grief to her children and grandchildren. As it became clear that a full cure was unlikely to occur, she began to think and speak more about her death and how to prepare herself and her family for it.

I remember vividly how she said to me one day, "I am not afraid to die. I feel safe in God's love. I know that you and many others pray for me every day and that nothing bad can happen to me. But I worry about the kids." As she said this, she began to cry. I knew how close she felt to her grandchildren, Charles and Sarah, and how much their lives, their happiness, and their future concerned her. I asked her, "What are you thinking?" She said, "I don't want the kids to suffer because of me. I don't want them to become sad and sorrowful as they see me dying. They always knew me as the strong grandmother they could count on. They don't know me as a paralyzed woman whose hair is falling out because of radiation therapy. I worry when I look into their faces and see them so anxious and sad. I want them to be happy children now and after I am gone." Connie didn't think about herself. She thought first of others. She wanted to be sure that I would find a good person to take over her work in the office. She wanted to be sure that her illness would not interrupt the life of her children and their families. Most of all, she wanted her grandchildren to be happy people. She worried that her sickness and death would prevent that.

As I saw Connie's pain, I saw more than ever what a beautiful, generous, caring person she is. She deeply cares for all the people who are part of her life. *Their* well-being is more important for her than her own. *Their* work, *their* pleasures, and *their* dreams concern her more than her own. In this society, in which most people are so self-centered, Connie is a true ray of light.

Still, I wanted Connie to move beyond her worries and to trust that her love for her family and friends would be fruitful. I wanted her to believe that what was important was not only what she did or still could do for others, but also—and ever-more so—what she lives in her illness and how she lives it. I wanted her to come to see that, in her growing dependence, she is giving more to her grandchildren than during the times when she could bring them in her car to school, to shops, and to sports fields. I wanted her to discover that the times when she needs them are as important as the times when they need her. In fact, in her illness, she has become their real teacher. She speaks to them about her gratitude for life, her trust in God, and her hope in a life beyond death. She shows them real thankfulness for all the little things they do for her. She doesn't keep her tears or fears hidden when they suddenly well up, but she always returns to a smile.

Connie herself can't see most of her own goodness and love. But I and the many other people who visit her can see it. Now, in her growing weakness, she who lived such a long and productive life gives what she couldn't give in her strength: a glimpse of the truth that love is stronger than death. Her grandchildren will reap the full fruits of that truth.

In our dying, we become parents of generations to come. How true this is of many holy people. Through their weakness, they have given us a view of God's grace. They are still close to us: St. Francis of Assisi, Martin Luther, John Henry Newman, Thérèse de Lisieux, Mahatma Gandhi, Thomas Merton, John XXIII, Dag Hammarskjöld, Dorothy Day, and many who have belonged to our own little circle of family and friends. Our thoughts and feelings, our words and writings, our dreams and visions are not just our own, they belong also to the many men and women who have died already and are now living within us. The lives and deaths of these people are still bearing fruit in our lives. Their joy, hope, courage, confidence, and trust haven't died with them but continue to blossom in our hearts and the hearts of the many who are connected with us in love. Indeed, these people keep sending the Spirit of Jesus to us and giving us the strength to be faithful in the journey we have begun.

We, too, must see to it that our deaths become fruitful in the lives of those who will live after us. Without care, however, it is difficult, if not impossible, to let our lives bear fruit in the generations to come. Devoid of care, our society makes us believe that we are what we have, what we do, or what people think about us. With such a belief, our death is, indeed, the end because, when we die, all property, success, and popularity vanishes. Without care for each other, we forget who we truly are—children of God and each other's brothers and sisters—and so cannot become parents of generations to come. But as a community of care, we can remind each other that we will bear fruit far beyond the few years we have to live. As a community of care, we trust that those who live long after we have lived will still receive the fruits of the seeds we have sown in our weakness and find new strength from them. As a community of care, we can send the Spirit of Jesus to each other. Thus we become the fruit-bearing people of God who embrace past, present, and future and thus are a light in the darkness.

Our meals in the Daybreak community show something about fruitfulness born in weakness. Meals in our houses are the high points of our daily life. They are like small celebrations. Food is eaten slowly, because many of us cannot eat by ourselves and need to be fed. Conversations around the table are simple, because many of us cannot speak, and those who can don't use many words. Prayers are always for others; each person is mentioned by name because, for people with mental disabilities, other people are what really count. Often there are candles and flowers, and on special occasions there are banners and balloons.

Whenever I am part of such a meal, I become acutely aware that the gifts of the Spirit of Jesus are given to us in weakness. Even while many of us experience much physical or emotional pain, while quite a few cannot make a move without assistance, and while some have few ways to communicate needs and desires, the spiritual gifts of peace, joy, gentleness, forgiveness, hope, and trust are very much present. Our shared vulnerability seems to be the favorite climate for Jesus to show us his love, for it is certainly not we who have created these gifts of love. We wouldn't even know how to go about doing such a thing. Many of us are too preoccupied with just surviving or helping others to survive. As in all families and communities, there are tensions and conflicts, too. Still, it seems that around this table of poverty, Jesus becomes powerfully present, generously sending his spirit.

During the time of prayer at the end of each meal, it becomes clear that these Daybreak meals have the quality of a memorial. We lift up not only our own life to God in gratitude, but also the lives of those of whose weaknesses we are aware, and especially the lives of those who are dying or have died. Thus we make all part of our "fellowship of weakness."

These memorial meals are also ways in which we care for each other and prepare each other to accept our final vulnerability. There is little chance that anyone will ever talk about our evening dinners as "last suppers," but still we want to say to each other, "When I am no longer here, keep remembering me whenever you come together to eat, drink, and celebrate, and I in return will send you the Spirit of Jesus, who will deepen and strengthen the bonds of love that bind you together." So every meal in which we remember Jesus and those who have died in him also prepares us for our own death. Thereby we not only feed ourselves, but also nurture each other, and so we become, each day, a little more the community of care to which we always will belong.

The Choice to Care Well

TO CARE WELL FOR THE DYING, we must trust deeply that these people are loved as much as we are, and we must make that love visible by our presence; we must trust that their dying and death deepen their solidarity with the human family, and we must guide them in becoming part of the communion of saints; and finally, we must trust that their death, just as ours, will make their lives fruitful for generations to come. We must encourage them to let go of their fears and to hope beyond the boundaries of death.

Caring well, just as dying well, asks for a choice. Although we all carry within us the gift to care, this gift can become visible only when we choose it.

We are constantly tempted to think that we have nothing or little to offer to our fellow human beings. Their despair frightens us. It often seems better not to come close than to come close without being able to change anything. This is especially true in the presence of people who face death. In running away from the dying, however, we bury our precious gift of care.

Whenever we claim our gift of care and choose to embrace not only our own mortality, but also other people's, we can become a true source of healing and hope. When we have the courage to let go of our need to cure, our care can truly heal in ways far beyond our own dreams and expectations. With our gift of care, we can gently lead our dying brothers and sisters always deeper into the heart of God and God's universe.

The Grace of the Resurrection

NEARLY THREE WEEKS have passed since I started to write this book on dying well and caring well. Although I have, for the most part, kept to my hermitage on the third floor of Franz and Reny's house, I have traveled far and wide in my mind. I have been with Maurice and Connie in Canada, Richard in the United States, and Marina in Holland. I have "visited" countless people in Europe, Asia, Africa, and Latin America who are dying as the result of war, starvation, and oppression, and I have tried to embrace with my heart those who have lived and died but continue to inform and inspire me with their actions and words.

During all these extensive mental travels, I have tried to claim for myself as well as for others that we are children of God, sisters and brothers of each other, and parents of generations to come. I have attempted to explore the ways in which this spiritual identity offers us a vision not only of how to die well ourselves, but also of how to care well for others who are dying.

Now as I sit behind my desk writing this conclusion, I realize a question may have come to those reading these words: "What of the resurrection?" It surprises me that so far I have neither written about the resurrection nor felt a need to do so. This simply didn't seem an urgent question as I was writing. But the fact that the resurrection didn't present itself with great urgency does not mean that it isn't important. To the contrary, the resurrection is more important than any of the things of which I have written so far because the resurrection is the foundation of my faith. To write about dying and death without mentioning the resurrection is like writing about sailing without mentioning the wind. The resurrection of Jesus and the hope of our own resurrection have made it possible for me to write about dying and death in the way that I have. With Paul the apostle, I dare to say, "[I]f Christ is proclaimed as raised from the dead, how can some of you be saying that there is no resurrection of the dead? For, if the dead are not raised, neither is Christ, and if Christ has not been raised, your faith is pointless and you have not, after all, been released from your sins. In addition, those who have fallen asleep in Christ are utterly lost. If our hope in Christ has been for this life only, we are of all people the most pitiable" (1 Corinthians 15:12–19).

It hardly seems possible to have a stronger opinion about the resurrection than Paul expresses in these words, and I want to make Paul's words my own. Still, I have not yet written about the resurrection of Jesus and of ourselves. I think that my hesitation in writing about this is connected with my conviction that the resurrection of Jesus is a hidden event. Jesus didn't rise from the dead to prove to those who had crucified him that they had made a mistake or to confound his opponents. Nor did he rise to impress the rulers of his time or to force anyone to believe. Jesus' resurrection was the full affirmation of his Father's love. He showed himself only to those who knew about this love. He made himself known as the risen Lord only to a handful of his close friends. Probably no other event in human history has had such importance while at the same time remaining so unspectacular. The world didn't notice Jesus' resurrection; only a few knew, those to whom Jesus had chosen to show himself and whom he wanted to send out to announce God's love to the world just as he had done.

The hiddenness of Jesus' resurrection is important to me. Although the resurrection of Jesus is the cornerstone of my faith, it is not something to use as an argument, nor is it something to use to reassure people. It somehow doesn't take death seriously enough to say to a dying person, "Don't be afraid. After your death you will be resurrected as Jesus was, meet all your friends again, and be forever happy in the presence of God." This suggests that after death everything will be basically the same, except that our troubles will be gone. Nor does it take seriously Jesus himself, who did not live through his own death as if it were little else than a necessary passage to a better life. Finally, it doesn't take seriously the dying, who, like us, know nothing about what is beyond this time- and place-bound existence.

The resurrection does not solve our problems about dying and death. It is not the happy ending to our life's struggle, nor is it the big surprise that God has kept in store for us. No, the resurrection is the expression of God's faithfulness to Jesus and to all God's children. Through the resurrection, God has said to Jesus, "You are indeed my beloved Son, and my love is everlasting," and to us God has said, "You indeed are my beloved children, and my love is everlasting." The resurrection is God's way of revealing to us that nothing that belongs to God will ever go to waste. What belongs to God will never get lost—not even our mortal bodies. The resurrection doesn't answer any of our curious questions about life after death, such as, How will it be? How will it look? But it does reveal to us that, indeed, love is stronger than death. After that revelation, we must remain silent, leave the whys, wheres, hows, and whens behind, and simply trust.

On the occasion of his ninetieth birthday, my father gave an interview to a Dutch radio station. After the reporter had asked him many questions about his life and work, and even more about the current Dutch tax system—since that was my father's professional interest—he finally wanted to know what my father thought would happen to him after his death.

My father and I were both listening to the program as it was broadcast a week after it was made. I was obviously quite curious about what my father's answer would be to that last question. I heard him say to the reporter, "I have very little to say about it. I don't really believe that I will see my wife or friends again as we see each other now. I don't have any concrete expectations. Yes, there is something else, but when there is no time and space anymore, any word about that 'something else' wouldn't make much sense. I am not afraid to die. I don't desire to become one hundred years old. I just want to live my life now as well as I can and . . . when I die, well, then we will see!"

Maybe my father's belief, as well as his lack of belief, is best summarized in these last words: "Well, then we will see." His skepticism and his faith touch each other in these words. "Well, then we will see" can mean "Well, it's all up in the air" or "Well, we finally will see what we always wanted to see!" We will see God, we will see one another. Jesus was clear about that when he said, "Do not let your hearts be troubled. You trust in God, trust also in me. In my Father's house there are many places to live in. . . . I am going now to prepare a place for you and after I have gone and prepared you a place, I shall return to take you to myself, so that you may be with me where I am" (John 14:1–3). When Jesus appeared to Mary of Magdala near the empty tomb, he sent her out with the words "Go and find my brothers and tell them: I am ascending to my Father and your Father, to my God and your God" (John 20:17).

The risen Jesus, eating and drinking with his friends, revealed that God's love for us, our love for each other, and our love for those who lived before and who will live after us is not just a quickly passing experience, but an eternal reality transcending all time and space. The risen Jesus, showing his pierced hands, feet, and side to his friends, also revealed that all we have lived in our body during our years on earth—our joyful as well as our painful experiences—will not simply fall away from us as a useless cloak but will mark our unique way of being with God and each other as we make the passage of death.

"Well, then we will see" will probably always have a double meaning. As the father of the epileptic boy, who asked Jesus to heal his child, we will always have to say, "I believe. Help my unbelief" (Mark 9:25). Still, when we keep our eyes fixed on the risen Lord, we may find not only that love is stronger than death, but also that our faith is stronger than our skepticism.

Death: A Loss and a Gift

YESTERDAY AFTERNOON, just as I was finishing the conclusion of this book, Jean Vanier called me from Trosly, France. In a gentle way, he said, "Henri, Père Thomas died this morning." Père Thomas Philippe, a French Dominican priest, was Jean's spiritual father and the cofounder of L'Arche. He was a man aflame with love of Jesus, Jesus' Mother Mary, and all the "little" people of this world. Père Thomas, who inspired his student and friend Jean Vanier and encouraged Jean to leave his teaching position in Toronto and start a life with disabled people—this holy and humble Dominican priest is now dead.

Listening to Jean, I heard the voice of a man who had lost his mentor and has now to continue alone.

"What a loss for you!" I said. He replied, "Yes, a great loss for me and for L'Arche . . . but also a great gift."

Père Thomas's death is indeed a loss and a gift. A loss, because so many people, including myself, can no longer visit him and find new hope by just being with him. During the most difficult period of my life, when I experienced great anguish and despair, he was there. Many times, he pulled my head to his chest and prayed for me without words but with a spirit-filled silence that dispelled my demons of despair and made me rise up from his embrace with new vitality. Countless people have been willing to wait for hours in the vestibule of his little room to be with him. People in despair, people with great mental suffering, people agonizing about the choices they have had to make, people not knowing how to pray, people who couldn't believe in God, people with broken relationships, and, recently, people living with AIDS and looking for someone to help them die well. We all have lost our good shepherd, our "crook and staff" in this valley of darkness and wonder how to keep going without him.

But as Jean said, Père Thomas's death is a gift, too. Now his life can bear full fruit. Père Thomas suffered immensely. He suffered for the church he loved so much, especially when the church closed the international community of students he had founded and no longer allowed him to continue his work as university chaplain. He suffered great loneliness when he came to the little village of Trosly in the north of France and began to minister there to a group of young men with mental disabilities. He suffered during the long hours he spent in front of the blessed sacrament in his little chapel, wondering what Jesus wanted of him. And after having started L'Arche with Jean Vanier, he often suffered from feelings of being misunderstood and even rejected, especially when he saw developments taking place that were quite different from what he had expected. As he became older, he entered into an ever-deeper communion with Jesus on the cross and suffered with him great anguish and feelings of abandonment.

When, finally, Père Thomas could no longer be with so many people, he withdrew to the south of France, where he lived for a few years in hiddenness. There he died a few days after Jean had visited him and a few hours after his brother, Père Marie Dominique, had given him the Eucharist. That was yesterday, February 4, at one o'clock in the morning. As Jean said, Père Thomas's death is not only a loss, but a gift, too. It is the end of a great suffering and the beginning of a new fruitfulness in L'Arche, in the church, in society, and in the hearts of the many who mourn his death.

When I began to write this book, I wasn't thinking about Père Thomas, even though he has been my main spiritual guide since I came to L'Arche. Since his leaving Trosly, he had become so hidden that even I didn't always fully realize that he had not yet made the final passage. Now it dawns on me how immensely lonely he must have been during these last years, alone as Jesus was alone on Golgotha, "the place of the skull" (John 19:17). But since Jean's telephone call, he is here with me. He is so much God's beloved child, brother of all those he cared for, and father of so many who will receive life from hearing about him, listening to his tapes, and reading his books. Seldom have I met a man who loved so deeply and intensely. He was truly on fire with love. So much did he love that he dared to say to me, "When you can't sleep during the night, just think of me and you will be fine." He had such confidence in the Spirit of Jesus blazing in him that he didn't say, "Think of God" or "Think of Jesus" or "Think of the Spirit," but rather he said, "Think of me." It was this burning love that made him heal so many and suffer so much. It was this love that penetrated every part of his being and made him into a living prayer: a prayer with eyes, hands, and a mouth that could only see, touch, and speak of God. This love consumed him as it consumed Jesus and gave life as it was consumed. This love could not and cannot die, but can only grow and grow.

The death of Père Thomas is given to me today to end this book. Père Thomas was a great gift to Jean, to me, and to many others. Now he is a gift to all people. Now he can send the Spirit of Jesus to everyone, and the Spirit can blow where and when it pleases.

Tomorrow, Saturday, I will leave Freiburg to go to France. I had not thought I would leave so soon — I have only been here three weeks — but after Jean's call, I want to be in Trosly, where Père Thomas's body will be brought and buried. I no longer want to be by myself in my little apartment writing about dying well and caring well. I want to be with that great community of people, poor and rich, young and old, strong and weak, gathered around the body of the man who loved so much and has been loved so much. As I travel from Freiburg to Strassburg, from Strassburg to Paris, from Paris to Compiègne, and from there to Trosly, I will think my thoughts and pray my prayers in communion with Moe, Rick, Marina, Connie, and my father, but I will feel especially close to Thomas Philippe, that beautiful man in whom the Spirit of Jesus was so fully alive and active. And in that large crowd of people mourning and giving thanks while breaking bread together in his memory, I will know as never before that God indeed is love.

Five More
Henri Nouwen Classics

Available wherever books are sold